SCIENCE ACADEMY

STOP THAT RACECAR!

BY KIRSTY HOLMES

CRABTREE
PUBLISHING COMPANY
WWW.CRABTREEBOOKS.COM

CRABTREE
PUBLISHING COMPANY
WWW.CRABTREEBOOKS.COM

Author:
  Kirsty Holmes
Editorial director:
  Kathy Middleton
Editors:
  Madeline Tyler, Janine Deschenes
Proofreader:
  Petrice Custance
Graphic design:
  Ian McMullen
Prepress technician:
  Katherine Berti
Print coordinator:
  Katherine Berti

All images are courtesy of Shutterstock.com, unless otherwise specified. With thanks to Getty Images, Thinkstock Photo, and iStockphoto.

Front Cover: LightField Studioss, Swiss Studio, Twin Design

Interior: Background – TheBestGraphics. Arrows – Sasha Ka. Characters: Lewis – Cookie Studio. Dee Dee – LightField Studios. Kush: Gratsias Adhi Hermawan. Ling: GOLFX. Paige: Oleksandr Zamuruiev. Katie: LightField Studios. BudE – sdecoret. Professor Adams – HBRH. 6. Ice_AisberG, Alex Mit. 7. RVillalon. 11. Blazej Lyjak. grese Dean Clarke. 12. severija, Candy Mafia. 13. Wanchai Orsuk. 15. Javier Brosch. 19. Babich Alexander. 20–21. GA, Digital Storm, Wallenrock, TORWAISTUDIO, Facanv, InsectWorld. 23. Den Rozhnovsky, Sergey Ginak, marijaf

All facts, statistics, web addresses, and URLs in this book were verified as valid and accurate at time of writing. No responsibility for any changes to external websites or references can be accepted by either the author or publisher.

Library and Archives Canada Cataloguing in Publication

Title: Stop that racecar! / by Kirsty Holmes.
Other titles: Stop that boxcar!
Names: Holmes, Kirsty, author.
Description: Series statement: Science academy | Originally published under title: Stop that boxcar! King's Lynn: BookLife, 2020. | Includes index.
Identifiers: Canadiana (print) 20200357743 |
  Canadiana (ebook) 20200357751 |
  ISBN 9781427130563 (hardcover) |
  ISBN 9781427130600 (softcover) |
  ISBN 9781427130648 (HTML)
Subjects: LCSH: Motion—Juvenile literature. |
  LCSH: Dynamics—Juvenile literature.
Classification: LCC QC133.5 .H65 2021 | DDC j531/.11—dc23

Library of Congress Cataloging-in-Publication Data

Names: Holmes, Kirsty, author.
Title: Stop that racecar! / by Kirsty Holmes.
Description: New York : Crabtree Publishing Company, 2021. | Series: Science academy | Includes index. | Audience: Ages 6-9 | Audience: Grades 2-3 | Summary: "Bud-E is building a racecar out of a box to race in the Robot Racear Rally. Join the students of Science Academy as they help build Bud-E's car and learn about the forces that make it go-and stop! Simple sentences and easy-to-understand examples make learning about forces understandable and fun"-- Provided by publisher.
Identifiers: LCCN 2020045838 (print) |
  LCCN 2020045839 (ebook) |
  ISBN 9781427130563 (hardcover) |
  ISBN 9781427130600 (paperback) |
  ISBN 9781427130648 (ebook)
Subjects: LCSH: Motion--Juvenile literature. | Force and energy--Juvenile literature. | Friction--Juvenile literature.
Classification: LCC QC127.4 .H647 2021 (print) |
  LCC QC127.4 (ebook) | DDC 531/.11--dc23
LC record available at https://lccn.loc.gov/2020045838
LC ebook record available at https://lccn.loc.gov/2020045839

Crabtree Publishing Company

www.crabtreebooks.com   1–800–387–7650
Published by Crabtree Publishing Company in 2021
© 2020 BookLife Publishing Ltd.

Published in Canada
Crabtree Publishing
616 Welland Ave.
St. Catharines, Ontario
L2M 5V6

Published in the United States
Crabtree Publishing
347 Fifth Ave
Suite 1402-145
New York, NY 10016

Printed in the U.S.A./122020/CG20201014

CONTENTS

Words that are bold, like **this**, can be found in the glossary on page 24.

ATTENDANCE

Another day at Science Academy has begun. Time to take attendance! Meet class 201.

Lewis
Favorite subject:
Electricity

Dee Dee
Favorite subject:
Movement

Katie
Favorite subject:
Pulling forces

Ling
Favorite subject:
Pushing forces

Paige
Favorite subject:
Magnets

Ravi
Favorite subject:
Energy

4

Today's lesson is all about the forces that change and stop movement. The students will learn answers to these questions:

- What causes movement?
- How do forces change the speed of an object?
- What is **friction**?
- What stops a moving object?

Bud-E

Favorite subject:
Being helpful!

Science Academy is a school especially for kids who love science and solving problems! Do I hear the bell?

It is a very exciting day. Class 201 has entered Bud-E in the school robot race. The students must work together to build a racecar that is fast enough to win the race. Bud-E is dreaming of the big, shiny trophy!

I am very excited! Beep! Beep!

Each racecar must be built out of a cardboard box. Boxes are great for holding many objects... but they are not very fast.

We're going to need to make some changes.

The box does not move by itself. A force is needed to make it move. During recess, the classmates push the box as hard as they can. But with Bud-E inside, the box is hard to push. It does not move very fast.

It will take so much pushing to win this race!

I think I know what the problem is...

Dee Dee knows all about how objects move. She explains that objects keep moving unless something stops them. To stop a moving object, a stronger force needs to push or pull against it in the opposite direction. Friction also slows down or stops objects from moving.

A strong pulling force can make a dog stop moving forward.

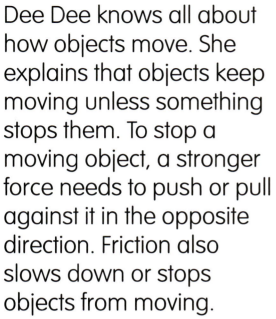

When you catch a baseball, you are using a pushing force to make the ball stop moving.

I think the box has a friction problem.

AFTERNOON LESSON

After lunch, Dee Dee takes the box to Professor Adams. She explains that she thinks friction is stopping the racecar from moving quickly. Professor Adams agrees.

Friction is a force created by two objects rubbing together. It makes objects slow down or stop moving.

The box creates friction when it slides across the floor. This slows it down. When Bud-E sits in the box, it moves even more slowly. That is because when the box is heavier, it creates more friction when it slides.

Even with a big push, friction will cause the box to stop moving.

11

Some objects, such as brakes on a car or bicycle, create a lot of friction. Others, such as slides and skis, create less friction. Rough objects create more friction than smooth objects.

Carpet

Have you ever tried to slide across a carpet? It is a **surface** that creates a lot of friction.

Glass

Smooth surfaces, such as glass, create less friction. Water glides easily down a window.

The racecar needs to be able to move without too much friction. The bottom of the box is smooth, but the road it will race on is rough. It makes too much friction.

The students need to find a way to make the box create less friction.

Dee Dee has a great idea! She remembered that her skateboard can move quickly on the road. That is because the skateboard has wheels! The wheels do not slide. They roll. This creates less friction.

Wheels create less friction when they move along the road. This lets my skateboard move quickly!

The classmates add some wheels to the box. Now, it moves more like a racecar! The wheels roll along. Bud-E is much faster now! But is the racecar fast enough?

I've done the math. I think we are still a few seconds too slow!

15

FRICTION IS ALL AROUND

The classmates wonder what is still causing the box to slow down. They solved the problem of friction on the bottom of the box. But there is more friction at work! Air hits the surface of a moving object and slows it down. This type of friction is called air **resistance**.

The larger a surface, the more air hits against it and slows it down.

A lot of air hits the flat, front surface of the box. This friction slows the box down.

Dee Dee tells her classmates that too much air is hitting the front of the box. They decide they need to make the car pointed at the front. If the front is pointed, there will be a smaller surface for air to hit. There will be less air resistance, so the car will move faster!

The air moves around the pointed end of the car instead of pushing against it.

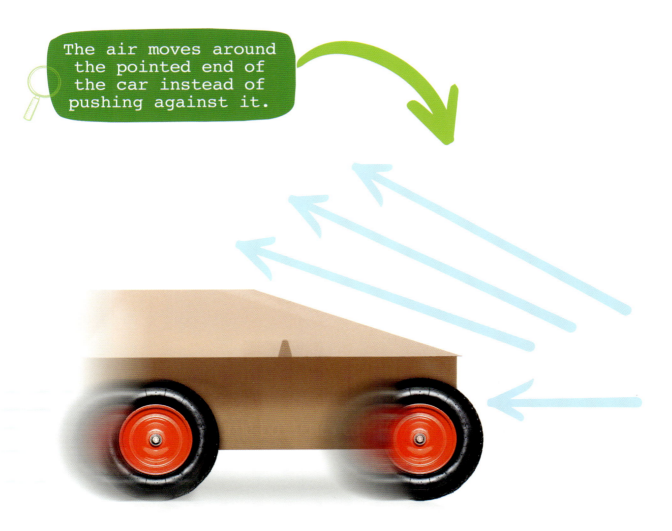

A WINNING DESIGN

The classmates make changes to the car. They give it a long, pointy shape so it won't be slowed down by air resistance. They even give Bud-E a comfortable seat.

> The box has **transformed** into a racecar! Good luck, Bud-E!

Pointed front
Less air resistance at the front

Together, the students of class 201 have **designed** a car that will create very little friction. Bud-E is sure he will win the race!

Long shape

Air will flow around the car instead of hitting flat surfaces

Wheels

Less friction below the car

HOW WILL IT STOP?

The classmates have one more problem to solve. How will the racecar stop? Dee Dee explains that it takes a force to stop something that is moving. There are a few ways the classmates can stop the racecar.

The classmates can put something strong but soft at the end of the road. It will create a pushing force on the car to make it stop.

The classmates can design brakes for the car. The brakes will squeeze on the wheels and make enough friction to make the car stop. Can you see the brakes on this bicycle wheel?

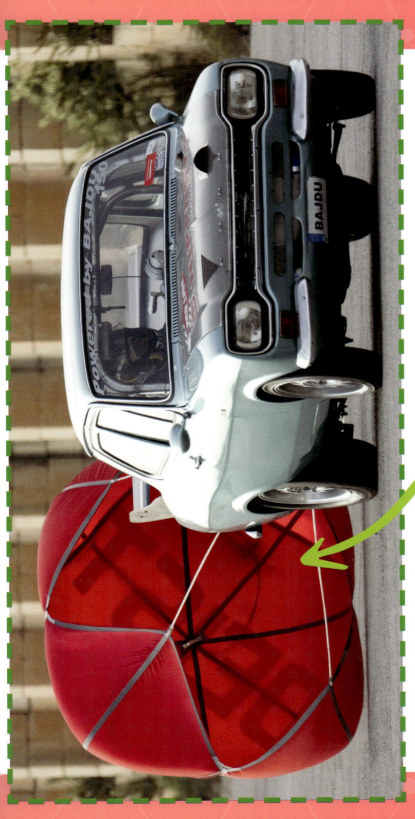

The classmates can add a **parachute** to the back of the car. The parachute has a large surface and causes a lot of air resistance. When it is time to stop, Bud-E can open the parachute.

The classmates decide that brakes are the best way to stop the racecar. Now, it is safe to drive! Can you think of other objects that use brakes to stop?

PROBLEM SOLVED

It worked! Dee Dee's advice made the racecar super fast. She also helped make sure it could stop safely. Bud-E and class 201 take home the trophy!

HOMEWORK

Look at the three moving objects below. Which forces are making each object move? How is friction changing how each object moves? How will each object stop? Talk about your answers with a classmate.

Skis

Sailboat

Bicycle

GLOSSARY

DESIGNED   Created based on a plan

FORCE   A push or pull that creates movement

FRICTION   A force that makes things slow down or stop moving. Friction is created when two objects rub together.

PARACHUTE   A cloth that fills with air and makes an attached object move more slowly

RESISTANCE   A slowing effect applied on one object by another, such as air on a car

SURFACE   The outer layer of something

TRANSFORMED   Fully changed

INDEX